The Hearse

FASTBACK® Horror

The Hearse

RICHARD LAYMON

GLOBE FEARON
Pearson Learning Group

FASTBACK® HORROR BOOKS

The Caller	The MD's Mistake
The Disappearing Man	Night Games
The Hearse	Night Ride
Live Bait	No Power on Earth
The Lonely One	The Rare Shell
The Masterpiece	Tomb of Horror

Cover Karen Beard/Stone/Getty Images. All photography © Pearson Education, Inc. (PEI) unless specifically noted.

Copyright © 2004 by Pearson Education, Inc., publishing as Globe Fearon®, an imprint of Pearson Learning Group, 299 Jefferson Road, Parsippany, NJ 07054. All rights reserved. No part of this book may be reproduced or transmitted in any form or by any means, electronic or mechanical, including photocopying, recording, or by any information storage and retrieval system, without permission in writing from the publisher. For information regarding permission(s), write to Rights and Permissions Department.

Globe Fearon® and Fastback® are registered trademarks of Globe Fearon, Inc.

ISBN 0-13-024514-3
Printed in the United States of America
2 3 4 5 6 7 8 9 10   07 06 05

Globe Fearon
Pearson Learning Group

1-800-321-3106
www.pearsonlearning.com

"Here's one for you, McCoy."

Tom Harris, sitting nervously on a chair near the office door, watched his new boss hand a sheet of paper to McCoy.

The big man spent a moment reading it. Then he grinned. "Ho, boy," he said.

"Any problem with that?" the boss asked.

"No sweat," McCoy answered.

"Well, it made Beamis sweat. I sent him for it last night and he flew the coop.

Probably went off and got himself a snootful. Hasn't shown his face around here since."

"Beamis never had much guts," McCoy said.

"Take Harris with you."

Tom sat up straight as McCoy turned to him. The man smiled in a way that made his stomach knot. Tom tried to smile back. At the thought of being alone with McCoy, he almost wished he hadn't taken the job.

McCoy looked fierce. Though he was young, no older than thirty, his head was hairless except for bushy brows that hung over his small, piggish eyes. He seemed to have no neck. His T-shirt, stretched tightly over bulging muscles, looked as though it would split apart if he took a deep breath. On the front of the shirt was the saying, "Don't get mad, get even."

"Are you Harris?" he asked.

"Yes sir," Tom said.

"This will be Harris's first job," the boss said. "I want you to show him the ropes."

"Glad to."

Tom didn't like the way he said that. Nor did he like the gleam in McCoy's tiny eyes.

"Okay," the boss said. "Get to it."

McCoy picked up a black tool box. Tom opened the office door for him, and followed him into the garage. They climbed into an old Plymouth, McCoy behind the wheel.

"So, kid, this is your first night?"

"Yes sir."

"Call me McCoy. None of this 'sir' stuff, got it?"

"Yes."

He drove out of the garage. The city streets were nearly deserted. "Ever steal a car before?" McCoy asked.

"No."

"I didn't think so. Well, it's a cinch. Always wanted to be a private eye, I'll bet."

"Yes."

"Well, this is as good a way to start as any. It's the bottom rung, repossessing cars, but somebody's got to do it. The world's full of flakes who buy stuff they can't afford. The way I see it, they're no better than thieves. And they call *us* thieves."

"They do?" Tom asked.

"Sure. They see you making off with their cars and they act like they own the things. I've been shot at, knifed. That's how come we work this time of night. If you're lucky, the jerks are sleeping and they don't give you any grief. Next thing they know, they wake up in the morning and their car's gone. Half the time, the creeps think they've been ripped off and call the cops."

"Do the police ever cause trouble?"

"Sure. If they catch you in the act. For all they know, you're just a crumb out to steal a car. It gets hairy sometimes. You're okay, though, once you show them the repo sheet. It's the owners you've got to worry about. *Owners.*" He snorted.

"They just *think* they're owners. But they really go crazy on you. Always keep an eye out for them. We had a guy last year who got caught repossessing a Jaguar and got himself wasted."

"Killed?" Tom asked.

"A twelve-gauge sawed-off shotgun will do that to a guy."

"Geez," Tom said, and tried not to sound too scared.

"Sound like the job's exciting enough for you?"

"Maybe too exciting."

"How's this for you?" McCoy asked, and pulled over to the curb. He pointed a thick finger across the street.

Parked in the driveway of the Green Fields Mortuary was a long, black hearse.

"**Y**ou're kidding," Tom said.

McCoy shined a small flashlight on the repo sheet. "I think that's our baby," he said. "A 1983 Chrysler limo, funeral model, purchased by a turkey, name of Uriah Stubbins. Owes better than eighteen thousand on it, and hasn't made a payment in three months." McCoy chuckled. "That's a good one," he said. "A funeral director who's a deadbeat."

Tom didn't feel like laughing. "We have to steal a *hearse*?"

"Not steal it, kid. We're taking possession for the lenders."

"But a hearse."

McCoy grinned at him. "Yeah, and I bet

it's carted plenty of stiffs to the bone orchard." He laughed some more, then climbed out of the car. He took his tool box from the back seat, and shut his door quietly. Tom stepped onto the curb and eased his own door shut.

He stared across the street. The lighted sign of Green Fields Mortuary cast a pale glow over the lawn. The building itself, partly hidden by a row of bushes, was dark at the windows. "Do you think he's in there?"

"Stubbins?" McCoy asked. "More than likely. If he's too cheap to pay for his hearse, he probably lives in a back room."

They walked to the other side of the street and started up the long driveway. "I wouldn't want to live in a place like this," Tom said.

"You're not a mortician. Those guys love their work. A house full of stiffs is just the ticket. I had a pal who used to work in one of these places. His boss lived in a back room and slept in a coffin."

"Yuck."

McCoy stopped behind the hearse. He shined his flashlight on the license plate, and checked the numbers against his repo sheet. "This is it, all right." His beam passed over the rear window, and Tom noticed curtains hanging inside.

"Okay," McCoy said, "let's take her." He shut off the light.

They stepped to the driver's door. McCoy scanned the front of the dark mortuary. Tom followed his gaze as he looked at the street. No cars were coming. "Keep a sharp eye out, kid."

Tom watched the street and building, but kept glancing at McCoy. The big man tried the door. It was locked. He crouched and opened his tool box. He took out a long, slim bar that was curved at one end. He shoved the bent end through a gap at the edge of the door. With a flick of his wrist, he popped up the lock button.

"A cinch, huh?"

"Yeah."

"Half the time, you can't get in this way. You've got to pick the lock. Do you know how to do that?"

Tom nodded. "I took locksmith training."

"Good. Then you know all about it. You'll be in fine shape, as long as you don't run into a Cadillac. I spent four hours one night trying to bust into a Caddy. Never did get in."

He picked up his tool box, opened the door of the hearse, and sat behind the steering wheel.

Tom glanced at the mortuary. Its windows were still dark. He saw no one. He looked up and down the street. "Did you give up on the Cadillac?" he asked.

"Not me. Waited till the creep came out to get in, and asked for his keys."

"Did he give you any trouble?"

"He was gutless. Do you know how to pull an ignition, kid?"

"Yes."

"Sure easier than hot-wiring. Out goes the old, in goes the new."

Bending over, Tom watched McCoy take

an ignition unit from his tool box and crank it into a hole on the steering column. "Nothing to it," the man said. He turned the key and the engine started with a smooth, quiet purr. He left the engine running, packed up his tools, and stepped out.

"She's all yours, kid."

Tom's heart raced. "Mine?"

"One of us has to drive this back to the garage. You're it. I'll take the car."

Tom did not want to get into the hearse. But he didn't want to seem cowardly in front of McCoy. "Fine," he muttered.

He sat on the driver's seat and reached for the door handle. McCoy was already striding toward the street. He pulled the door shut. He released the emergency brake. He wiped his sweaty hands on his jeans, and pushed the shift to reverse.

He took a deep, shaky breath. The air smelled like flowers. He groaned.

I bet it's carted plenty of stiffs to the bone orchard.

Quickly, he rolled down his window and took a deep breath of fresh air.

Then he backed the hearse slowly down the driveway.

As the rear tires bumped onto the road, a quick pounding noise came from behind. Tom jumped with fright and hit the brake.

"Lucky you," McCoy said, stepping up to the window. "The heap's got a flat."

"You want help changing it?"

He shook his head. "No spare. We'll have to leave it and worry about it later."

Tom sighed with relief as McCoy walked around the front of the hearse. He unlocked the passenger door, and the big man climbed in.

"I'll bet you're glad for the company, huh?"

Tom shrugged. "Either way is fine with me." Already, he could feel his heart slowing down. He was *very* glad for the company.

He backed onto the street, shifted to drive, and sped away from Green Fields Mortuary.

"Clean as a whistle," McCoy said. "Poor Uriah is going to wake up tomorrow and wonder what hit him."

"I hope he doesn't have a funeral," Tom said. His voice sounded a little shaky.

"Wouldn't that be a shame? It would serve the deadbeat right. Let him shove the stiff in a taxi."

Tom laughed.

"Stinks in here," McCoy said. "Enough to turn you off flowers." He rolled down his window. He settled back, turned toward Tom, and rested an elbow on the top of his seat. "What's your name, kid?"

"Tom."

"Well, Tom, you did real good for your first time out. You've got guts. I like that. Lots of guys, they wouldn't be caught dead in a hearse." McCoy chuckled at his little joke, and Tom smiled.

"Next time around, I'll stand watch and

we'll see how good you are at heisting cars."

"That'd be great."

"If you ask me, you've got what it takes. Having the guts, that's half the battle in this line of work. Hank, he'll keep you doing repos for a while. Next thing you know, he'll have you doing investigations. Then you can break out your deerstalker hat and make like Sherlock Holmes."

"I'm all for that."

"Yep."

Tom stopped at a traffic light.

McCoy looked over his shoulder. "Nice curtains." He reached back and touched them. "Velvet," he said. "Real nice." Then he swept the curtains open. "Well, what do you know? We've got company."

Twisting around, Tom peered into the

rear of the hearse and saw the dim shape of a coffin.

"How about that?" McCoy said. He sounded amused.

Tom was not at all amused. His heart was thudding hard. His stomach felt cold and tight. His mouth was as dry as sand. Afraid that his voice would sound shaky, he took a deep breath and said loudly, "What'll we do?" His voice sounded better than he thought it would.

"You'd better pull over. Hank isn't going to want a stiff in his garage."

"A stiff?"

"Sure. You don't think the coffin's empty, do you?"

"It might be," Tom said. He sure hoped so.

"Empty or not, we've got no rights to the coffin."

The light changed. Tom drove through the intersection and stopped at a curb in front of a closed hardware store. "Now what?" he asked.

"No choice, Tom. We've got to take the coffin back to Uriah."

"What's it *doing* in here at this time of night?"

"Maybe an early funeral, who knows?"

"Geez."

McCoy laughed softly. "Does it spook you, riding with a stiff?"

"Who, me?" Tom forced a laugh. "No sweat, as long as it stays in the coffin."

"Yeah. That'd be something if it snuck

up here and grabbed us. What do they call them, zombies?"

Tom nodded.

"Ever seen a dead guy?"

"Not yet."

"Here's your big chance."

"You're joking."

"You're not chicken, are you?"

"No, but . . ."

"What-say we open up the box and take a peek?"

"We can't do that," Tom said, trying to keep the fear out of his voice.

"Why not? Who's going to find out?"

"It . . . it's just not right. We shouldn't fool around with someone who's dead."

"If he complains, we'll tell him we're sorry. Come on. Aren't you curious? It's not every night you get a chance to take a good look at a stiff. It'll do you good. You ever hear of a squeamish private eye?"

"No, but . . ."

"See if you can put some light on the subject."

Tom twisted the headlight knob. The dashboard brightened. He turned the knob more. It made a quiet click and an overhead light came on. He looked over his shoulder. A row of lights on the rear ceiling cast a yellowish glow onto the coffin.

It was made of dark, polished wood with shiny handles along each side.

"We shouldn't," Tom said.

McCoy winked at him. "Come on, Tom." Then he took his tool box off the floor. He climbed over the top of his seat, and crawled toward the coffin.

Tom groaned. He saw himself leaping into the street and running away. But if he did that, he would never again be able to face McCoy.

"Are you just going to sit there?" McCoy said.

Turning around, he squirmed over the back of the seat. On hands and knees, he made his way to the coffin.

McCoy was already busy loosening screws along the lid. "Give me a hand," he said. Tom searched through the tool kit, found another screwdriver, and crawled to the other side of the coffin.

He was shaking badly. He had a hard time fitting the tip into the slotted head of the first screw, and finally used one hand to hold the blade steady while he twisted the driver. The screw turned easily. When it was loose, he moved sideways to the next one.

McCoy grinned at him. "Ten bucks says it's a guy."

"What makes you think so?" Tom asked.

"Nothing. Just that a bet always spices things up. How about it? Even money. I say it's a guy, you say it's a gal."

"Well, all right."

They finished with the screws. McCoy knelt at the foot of the coffin, Tom at its head.

"All set?" McCoy asked.

"Ready."

They lifted the lid and shoved it aside. McCoy suddenly jerked as if he'd been kicked in the back. His tiny eyes opened wide. "Holy *smoke*," he muttered.

Tom looked into the coffin. Stretched out inside was a young man dressed in jeans and a dirty blue shirt. His blond hair was a wild tangle. There was a stubble of whiskers on his chin. His eyes were shut, but his mouth hung open.

Staring down at him, Tom felt sick.

McCoy was gasping as if he had trouble getting enough air into his lungs.

"Are you okay?" Tom whispered.

McCoy wiped a hand over the top of his bald head. "Man," he said.

"Yeah. I guess you win the ten bucks. Can we cover him up now?"

McCoy shook his head. "It's . . . it's . . ." His face suddenly went pale.

Tom looked down at the body.

Its eyes suddenly opened.

A low moan came from its mouth.

Tom sprang away. His head slammed the ceiling. He dropped to his knees and tumbled toward the open coffin as the body lurched up.

With McCoy at one end and Tom at the other, they carried the coffin up the dark walkway to the front door of Green Fields Mortuary McCoy let go with one hand, and pressed the doorbell. Chimes rang inside.

They waited.

McCoy rang the bell again.

Finally a porch light came on and the door swung open. A lean man looked out at them with sunken eyes. He wore pajamas and a robe. His black hair was slicked down as if he'd taken time to comb it before answering the door. He frowned when he saw the coffin.

"Uriah Stubbins?" McCoy asked.

"Yes. What . . ?"

"We got your coffin by mistake."

"I'm afraid I don't . . ." He backed out of the doorway as McCoy stepped toward him. "What are you doing?"

"Bringing it in for you."

Just inside the door, they dropped the coffin to the rug. Uriah started to turn away, but McCoy grabbed him.

Tom flung the lid off the coffin. It was empty.

"We've got a surprise for you," McCoy told the struggling undertaker.

Through the front door stepped a blond man in jeans and a dirty blue work shirt.

"What were you going to do?" McCoy asked Stubbins. "Bury him alive? You crud. He was just trying to do his job, and you tried to kill him."

"I caught him last night!" Stubbins cried out. "He was trying to steal my hearse!"

"Not steal it," McCoy said. "Repossess it. You should've paid your bills."

Beamis stopped in front of Uriah. His fist shot into the skinny man's belly. Uriah went down quickly.

As Tom watched, McCoy and Beamis lifted the gasping man. They dropped him into the coffin. Beamis held him down while Tom and McCoy picked up the lid and put it in place. It muffled Uriah's screams.

Beamis sat on top of the lid, grinning, while Tom and McCoy screwed it down.

"Let's go," McCoy finally said. "We'll leave him like that for awhile and then call someone to let him out."

"Yeah, but we'll let him sweat in there first," Beamis said.

The three men left the coffin inside Green Fields Mortuary and walked through the cool night air toward the waiting hearse. McCoy slapped Tom on the back. "You've got what it takes, pal. Guts."